Scone Recipes:

Amazing Scone Baking Race

Premium Tea Room Scones Recipes

Including Prize-Winning Scones Recipes

From the Kitchens of Bakers and Judges

At the Amazing Scone Baking Contests

Scone Recipes:

Amazing Scone Baking Race

Premium Tea Room Scones Recipes

Delicious, Prize-Winning Recipe Collection

From the Kitchens of Bakers and Judges

At the Amazing Scone Baking Contests

50+ Amazing Scone Recipes
to delight the baker insider of you
and to serve with pride at any
cream tea or afternoon tea.
Perfect for traditional and vintage tearooms!
Jennifer C. Petersen and Friends

Judie Stanton, Editor

ISBN-13: 978-1492341543
ISBN-10: 1492341541

Traditional Baking Skills

A traditional part of British afternoon tea, this Scottish quick bread is said to have taken its name from the Stone of Destiny (or Scone), the place where Scottish kings were once crowned. The original triangular-shaped scone was made with oats and griddle-baked.

Americanized versions are more often flour-based and baked in the oven. They come in various shapes including triangles, rounds, squares and diamonds. Scones can be savory or sweet and are usually eaten for breakfast and almost always served at tea and in coffee shops.

Although the correct way to pronounce scone, following the Queen's English, is "scahn" to rhyme with dawn or fawn [Br. SKON], in parts of Great Britain and America, it is pronounced scohn [SKOHN] to rhyme with moan or groan as in "that's a lower class pronunciation.....groan".

Either way, scones are an appreciated treat or as you can see from the following recipes, each baker has a favorite way of tweaking scone recipes. In the old days, scones were somewhat plain. For celebrations and other special occasions, embellishments were added including fruit, nuts, spices and mashed potatoes. In today's culture, we seem to take the additions as commonplace and become more adventuresome with the addition of ingredients such as chocolate chips, cheese, and ground tea leaves or tea infusions.

Several of these recipes call for a citrus zest. Zest is the finely shredded outer skin of the fruit. Avoid using any of the white pithy part of the skin as it will add a bitter flavor.

Top 10 Tips for Baking Amazing Scones

1. **Dry Ingredients:** Use fresh ingredients (especially baking soda and baking powder) as they are essential to making amazing scones. Always measure first and then sift the flour and dry ingredients. Sifting adds lightness and removes large lumps.

2. **Equipment:** Keep all your equipment (bowls, utensils, and working surface) and ingredients cold. Cold and colder but coldest is best.

3. **Butter:** Use butter only and use it straight from the refrigerator. Cut into small cubes, and then add to the flour mixture.

4. **Kneading:** Knead gently until dough just comes together. Don't over mix or over handle the dough as will make your scones tough and dry. Some baking instructors advise not using a food processor for cutting the butter and flour mixture, but I have no opposition to it.

5. **Folding Option:** The letter folding option - For flakey, layered scones, use a folding technique. Roll the dough out to about 3/8-inch thick. Fold the dough in half and in half and repeat again. Roll the dough out to about ¾-inch thick before cutting the scones. In the oven, the butter bits form pockets of steam and give scones their light and flaky texture.

6. **Rolling and Cutting:** Lightly dust your work surface. Don't use too much flour or it alters the recipe. Use a sharp, floured cutter on dough. Do not twist the cutter as it causes unevenly risen, lopsided scones. Scones can be cut into various shapes:

round, heart, diamond, squares or triangles. Dip the edges of the cutter in flour to prevent the dough from sticking. Wedge or triangular cuts are the simplest and fastest. Form dough into a round and using a knife dusted with flour, cut into triangles. Brush with cream.

7. **Sugaring:** Sprinkling sugar on scones before baking adds an extra touch of sweetness and texture. Try granulated, sanding or raw sugar for different textures and finishes.

8. **Baking**: Preheat the oven. A hot oven is essential to cook evenly risen, golden-brown scones. Prepare the baking sheet by lining with parchment paper; use a Silpat (silicone baking mat), or grease lightly. Place ¼" apart.

9. **Finish with a Flourish:** Immediately remove from the baking sheet to cool on wire racks. A hot baking sheet will continue to cook the scones and may make a hard crust. Drizzle with a glaze or brush with melted butter if not using sanding sugar.

10. **Host with the Most:** Make scones up to the point where you've shaped them and put them on the baking sheet. Don't brush with topping or cream. Instead, tent with plastic wrap and put them in the freezer. When they're totally frozen, put them in a plastic bag, and seal the bag. When ready to bake, preheat your oven to 425°F, and take the scones out of the freezer. Put them on a lightly greased or parchment-lined baking sheet, and brush with cream. Frozen scones take extra baking time – allow an extra 20 to 25 minutes. (By the

way, I don't recommend freezing scones for entering into the Amazing Scone Baking Race since you want the freshest scones possible for the baking contest.) Scones should be eaten within a couple of hours of baking so for baking contest purposes, try to bake as soon before judging time as possible.

Happy Baking! And may all your scones be light and fluffy!   Jennifer

Table of Contents

Almond Sultana Scones

2013 Blue Ribbon Winner - Oregon State Fair - Baker: Nancy Baker-Krofft

2 cups King Arthur all-purpose flour
½ cup King Arthur white whole-wheat flour
¼ cup sugar
½ tsp. salt
1 Tbsp. baking powder
1 cup almond meal
2 whole eggs, beaten
½ cup cold butter, diced
1 tsp. almond extract
1 cup sliced almonds
¼ cup golden sultana raisins
about ¼ cup clabbered cream (or soured half- &- half cream)

Procedure

Preheat oven to 350°F. Line a baking sheet with parchment paper or a Silpat. In a large mixing bowl, sift together the dry ingredients. Using your fingers, mix in the cold butter.

In a liquid measuring cup, beat the eggs. Add clabbered cream (or soured half-and-half*) to beaten eggs so that together they measure one cup. Add almond extract and stir well. Add egg mixture to dry ingredients; fork together. Add almonds and raisins. Chill for 30 minutes.

On a floured work surface, shape and flatten the dough into a circle. Cut into 8 portions and transfer to prepared baking sheet. Bake at 350°F for 20 to 22 minutes or until golden brown. Cool on rack.

(*Soured half-and-half: Add 1 tsp. vinegar to 1-cup half-and-half.)

America's Best Gluten Free Scones

1 ¾ cups King Arthur Gluten-Free Multi-Purpose Flour
¼ cup sugar
2 tsp. baking powder
½ tsp. xanthan gum
½ tsp. salt
¼ tsp. nutmeg, optional
½ cup cold butter
¾ cup diced dried apricots, cherries, currants or cranberries
2 large eggs
1/3 cup cold milk
1 tsp. gluten-free vanilla extract

Procedure

Preheat the oven to 400°F. Grease a baking sheet or line with Silpat or parchment paper.

Whisk together the flour, sugar, baking powder, xanthan gum, salt, and nutmeg. Cut in the cold butter until the mixture is crumbly. Stir in the dried fruit.

Whisk together the eggs, milk, and vanilla till frothy. Add to the dry ingredients, stirring till well blended. The dough cling together and will be very sticky.

Drop scone dough by ¼ cupful or use a small cookie scoop onto the baking sheet. Let the scones rest for about 15 minutes.

Sprinkle the scones with baking sugar crystals or cinnamon sugar, if desired. Bake for 15 to 20 minutes or until golden brown. Remove from the oven and let rest for 5 minutes before serving. Delicious when served warm with jam and clotted cream. Makes about 8 scones.

Autumn Days Scone Bites

2013 White Ribbon Winner - Clark County Fair - Youth - Andrea Beauchamp

3 ½ cups King Arthur bread flour
½ cup white sugar
2 Tbsp. baking powder
1 tsp. baking soda
½ tsp. salt
¼ tsp. nutmeg
1 cup cold butter, finely diced
1 whole egg beaten
1 cup milk
¾ cup cooked pumpkin

1/3 cup cocoa powder
2 whole apples - peeled, cored, and chopped
¼ cup golden brown sugar, packed
¼ cup sliced almonds

Icing
1 cup confectioners' sugar, sifted
6 Tbsp. butter, melted
1 tsp. vanilla extract
¼ cup milk

Procedure

Preheat oven to 400°F. Lightly grease a cookie sheet with butter. In a large bowl, combine flour, sugar, cocoa, baking powder, salt, nutmeg, baking soda and sliced almonds. Cut in butter. Set aside.

Dice two medium apples and set aside. In a small saucepan, melt two tablespoons butter with golden brown sugar. Add the apples to the saucepan and simmer until apples are coated and become slightly mushy. Once completed, set aside to cool.

Mix the egg and milk in a small bowl then stir into flour mixture until just moistened. Add cooked pumpkin and fold in until well mixed.

Over a strainer, pour the apple mixture into a bowl and hold there until all the excess sugar/butter coating has come off the apples. Add the apples to the scone mixture and stir until mixed in.

Drop 16 large spoonsful of dough onto the greased cookie sheet and bake in 400°F oven for 17 minutes or until edges are golden brown.

Icing

While the scone bites are baking, melt 6 tablespoons of butter. In a small bowl, combine confectioner's sugar and melted butter until mixture becomes sticky. Add vanilla extract and milk, stirring until it is a thin icing.

Presentation

Allow scones to cool for two minutes, and then cut into bite-sized triangles for easy eating. Drizzle the icing over the scones using a spoon or whisk. Enjoy!

Black Tea Lemon Scones

Red Ribbon - 2011 - Oregon State Fair   Baker: Renata Stanko

1 ½ cup old-fashioned oatmeal
1 ½ cup buttermilk, chilled
1 ½ cup King Arthur unbleached all-purpose flour
2 Tbsp. sugar
2 tsp. baking soda
1 ½ tsp. salt
1 tsp. lemon peel, grated
6 Tbsp. unsalted butter
1 tsp. lemon extract
2 Tbsp. strong infused English Breakfast tea, cold

Glaze
3 Tbsp. powdered sugar, sifted
2 tsp. strong infused English Breakfast tea, cold

Procedure

Combine oatmeal and buttermilk. Refrigerate overnight.

Preheat oven to 425°F. Sift together the flour, sugar, baking soda and salt. Stir in grated lemon peel. Cut in butter until crumbly.

Add oatmeal mixture, lemon extract and tea. Fold into a ball and place on floured surface. Pat into a circle ½ inch thick. Cut into 12 wedges. Bake for 12 to 14 minutes or until light golden brown. Remove from oven and drizzle with glaze.

Glaze Stir together the powdered sugar and tea. Mix well.

Blueberry Lime Scones

1 ½ cups King Arthur Flour unbleached all-purpose flour
3 Tbsp. sugar
2 ½ tsp. baking powder
½ tsp. baking soda
¼ tsp. salt
2 tsp. lime zest
5 Tbsp. unsalted butter, cold and diced

½ cup dried blueberries
2/3 cup low-fat buttermilk

Glaze
¼ cup lime juice, freshly squeezed
1 cup powdered sugar, sifted
2 tsp. lime zest
½ Tbsp. unsalted butter

Procedure

Preheat oven to 400°F. In a large bowl, sift together the flour, sugar, baking powder, baking soda and salt. Stir in the lime zest. Use clean hands to mix butter into dry mixture until it resembles coarse meal. Lightly stir in dried blueberries.

Make a well in the center of the mixture. Add buttermilk and stir until combined; do not over mix. Transfer dough to a lightly floured surface; shape into an 8-inch round. Transfer to a baking sheet. Cut circle into 8 wedges; move them apart from each other. Bake until golden, about 18 to 20 minutes.

Cool slightly and drizzle with glaze.

Glaze

Mix the lime juice and sifted confectioners' sugar together in a microwave-safe bowl. Stir until the sugar dissolves. Add the lime zest and butter. Microwave for 20 seconds on high. Whisk the glaze to smooth out any lumps, and then drizzle the glaze over the top of the scones. Let the glaze set before serving. Can be stored up to three days in an airtight container.

Blueberry Scones 2011

2011 Blue Ribbon Winner - Oregon State Fair   Baker: Ruth Brown Peterson

4 cups King Arthur unbleached all-purpose flour
6 Tbsp. sugar
4 ½ tsp. baking powder
½ tsp. salt
½ cup + 2 Tbsp. cold unsalted butter, cut into pieces
2 large eggs slightly beaten
¾ cup + 2 Tbsp. milk, divided
1 ½ cups fresh or frozen blueberries

Procedure

Preheat oven to 375°F. Grease a baking sheet. In a bowl, combine the flour, sugar, baking powder and salt; cut in butter until mixture resembles coarse crumbs. In a bowl, whisk eggs and ¾-cup milk; add to dry ingredients just until moistened. Turn onto a lightly floured surface; gently knead in the blueberries.

Divide the dough in half. Pat each portion into an 8-inch circle; cut each circle into six or eight wedges. Place on greased baking sheets. Brush with remaining milk. Sprinkle with cinnamon sugar if desired.

Bake at 375°F for about 15 to 20 minutes or until tops are golden brown. Serve warm. Yield: 12 or 16 scones.

Blueberry Scones 2012

2012 Clark County Fair - Baker: Shelley Baldwin

4 cups all-purpose flour
3 Tbsp. sugar
4 tsp. baking powder
½ tsp. salt
½ tsp. cream of tartar
¾ cup butter
1 large egg, separated
1 ½ cups half-and-half

1 cup blueberries
Additional sugar

Glaze:
1/3 cup butter melted & cooled
2 cups confectioner's sugar
2 Tbsp. warm water
1 tsp. vanilla extract

Procedure

Preheat oven to 425°F. Line baking sheet with parchment paper or Silpat. Combine first 5 ingredients. Cut in butter with a pastry blender for 5 minutes or until coarse crumbs form.

Separate egg and add yolk to half-and-half; beat well. Add egg/half-and-half mixture to dry mixture; blend with fork to form soft dough.

On a floured work surface, knead 5 to six times. Poke in berries gently.

Divide dough into halves and pat each half into a 7" round. Cut each round into 6 wedges and brush with beaten egg white. Sprinkle with sugar.

Bake at 425°F for 15 to 20 minutes or until golden brown.

Glaze - Mix melted butter, sugar, water and vanilla extract until smooth. Drizzle over warm scones.

Makes 6 scones.

Candied Orange and Golden Raisin Scones

½ cup candied orange peel or citron, diced
½ cup golden raisins
1 tsp. grated orange peel
¼ cup Grand Marnier or other orange flavored liqueur
2 cups cake flour, sifted
1 ½ cups all-purpose flour plus more for rolling
¼ cup cold unsalted butter, cut into small cubes
½ cup sugar
5 tsp. baking powder
1 tsp. salt
1 cup cold heavy whipping cream
1 large egg slightly beaten
1 large egg, divided
Topping
1 large egg white, slightly beaten
Sanding sugar or large crystal sugar

Procedure

In a small bowl, stir together candied peel, raisins, orange zest and orange liqueur. Cover with plastic wrap and refrigerate for 1 day.

Preheat oven to 350°F. Line a baking sheet with parchment paper or Silpat. In a large bowl, sift together the flours. Transfer half to a food processor and add the butter. Pulse to cut in butter to small pea size. Add sugar, baking powder and salt to remaining flour in bowl; stir to combine. Work in flour-butter mixture until it resembles coarse meal.

In a large bowl, whisk together the heavy cream, whole egg and egg yolk. Make a well in the center of flour mixture and pour in half of cream mixture.

With a rubber spatula, using a figure 8 pattern, fold the dry ingredients over the wet ingredients, scraping bottom of bowl to incorporate all dry ingredients. Add remaining cream mixture and gently mix until dough just comes together. Do not over mix.

Turn out dough onto a lightly floured surface and press dough into a 6" x 9" rectangle. Sprinkle dried fruit mixture evenly over the dough. With a short side facing you, fold rectangle into thirds, like a letter fold. Rotate dough a quarter-turn clockwise. Roll out dough to a 6" x 9" rectangle, folding and rotating once more.

With floured hands, pat dough into a 1 ¼-inch thick rectangle. Using a 2" round cookie cutter, cut rounds from dough. Gather scraps, reroll once and cut more rounds (makes about 16 total).

Place scones 2" apart on prepared baking sheet. Lightly beat egg white and brush scone tops. Sprinkle with sanding sugar or coarse sugar.

Bake about 25 minutes or until golden brown, turning baking sheet halfway through. Remove from oven and let cool. Serve warm or at room temperature.

Recipe Notes

Thank you to Thistledown Cozies for sponsoring the Amazing Scone Baking Race!

A tea cozy is a cover for a teapot and is traditionally made of cloth. It insulates a teapot, keeping the tea warm. Thistledown Tea Cozies, "dedicated to keeping your tea hot," are insulated and come in many different patterns to coordinate with a teapot, tea table or desk.

Gift shops frequently carry tea cozies and if your favorite gift shop or tea room needs to stock tea cozies, please ask them to stock Thistledown Tea Cozies for you.

Thistledown Tea Cozies are made in the USA, are of the highest quality, and fully-lined in contrast fabric. Thick polyester batting offers superior heat retention. Machine wash and dry. Guaranteed to last through years of laundering. This is the best tea cozy with, fabulous fabrics and a true eye for design. Linings are color-coordinated.

Cheddar Bacon Jalapeño Scones

2013 White Ribbon Clark County Fair - Baker: Shelley Baldwin

4 cups King Arthur self-rising flour
1 tsp. cream of tartar
1 tsp. baking powder
1 tsp. baking soda
¼ tsp. white pepper
¼ cup cold butter, finely diced

6 oz. sharp cheddar cheese, grated; divided
2 cups milk
2/3 cup cooked and crumbled bacon bits
6 whole jalapeño peppers, seeded and minced

Procedure

Preheat oven to 425°F. Line baking sheet with parchment paper. In a large bowl, sift all dry ingredients together. Cut in butter until coarse cornmeal texture is achieved. Reserve ½ cup grated cheese and add the rest to the flour mixture. Add milk and stir until combined. Add additional milk if necessary to form a stiff dough.

Turn dough onto a floured surface. Roll dough to about 1-inch thickness; cut into desired shapes. Place on baking sheet. Bake in 425°F oven for 10 to 15 minutes or until lightly browned.

Choco Nutty Joy

Blue Ribbon Winner - Clark County Fair - 2011 Baker: Dale Groff

2 cups all-purpose flour
1/3 cup dark brown sugar; packed
1 tsp. baking powder
1 tsp. baking soda
2 Tbsp. buttermilk powder
½ tsp. salt
½ cup very cold butter, finely diced

1 extra-large egg
½ cup all-natural sour cream
1 tsp. coconut extract
1 cup dark chocolate chips (12 oz. pkg.)
½ cup almonds - slivered
1 cup shredded coconut, toasted

Procedure

Preheat oven to 400°F. Grease a baking sheet or line with parchment paper. In a large bowl, sift or whisk together the dry ingredients. Working quickly, add the very cold diced butter to the dry mixture. Stir lightly to create a crumbly texture of pea-size crumbs.

Add chocolate chips, slivered almonds and toasted coconut to the butter-flour mix.

In a separate bowl, mix the egg, sour cream and coconut extract. Mix well. Pour liquid into the dry mixture. Stir lightly with a fork or spatula then work with hands until the dough comes together into a ball.

Place ball on a floured surface and pat out into a 9-inch circle. Hug the edges around until the circle is about 8-inches around and 1 inch thick. Cut the circle in half, then into quarters. Cut each quarter twice forming twelve even triangles.

Place the pieces evenly on prepared baking sheet. Bake for 16 to 18 minutes at 400°F or until a golden brown color develops on top. Remove from oven and serve. Makes 12 scones.

Choco Scones

Clark County Fair - 2011 - Baker: Svetlana

¾ cup water, boiling
1 cup cocoa powder
6 large eggs, separated
1 cup sugar
½ cup butter
1 cup flour
1 Tbsp. baking powder

Procedure

Preheat oven to 350°F. Prepare an 11-inch baking pan with non-stick spray. Sift the cocoa powder into a small mixing bowl; add the boiling water stirring to avoid lumps. Set aside to cool.

Separate the eggs. Beat the egg whites gradually adding one-half of the sugar. Beat until stiff peaks form.

While egg whites are beating, in a separate mixing bowl, cream together the egg yolks and remaining sugar; gradually add the butter, flour and baking powder. Mix well. Pour the cooled cocoa into the egg batter and mix well.

By thirds, gently pour the batter into the stiff egg whites adding one-third cocoa mixture at a time. Fold gently in a figure-8 pattern. Pour the batter into a prepared baking pan; place in preheated oven. Bake for 40 minutes or until golden brown.

Remove from oven, cool for 10 minutes then transfer to a wire rack to completely cool. When cool, sprinkle with powdered sugar or cut into 3-inch squares and fill with cream filling or stabilized whip cream. Makes 12 scones.

Chocolate Chip Banana Bread Scones

2013 Clark County Fair - Baker: Tristann Graves

1 cup bananas, peeled and mashed (2 large)
¼ cup milk
½ cup plain yogurt
1 tsp. vanilla nut extract
2 ½ cups all-purpose flour
¼ cup granulated sugar
2 tsp. baking powder
½ tsp. salt
1 ½ tsp. ground cinnamon
4 Tbsp. unsalted butter

½ cup chocolate chips

Glaze
¼ cup milk
¼ cup creamy peanut butter
½ tsp. vanilla extract
1 ½ cups confectioner's sugar, sifted
¼ cup chopped walnuts, for garnish

Procedure

In a small bowl, mash the bananas and if needed add enough milk to make one cup. Stir in the milk, yogurt and vanilla nut extract.

In a large mixing bowl, sift the flour, sugar, baking powder, salt, and cinnamon together. Cut the butter into the dry ingredients using a fork, pastry cutter, or your fingertips until pieces are pea-size.

Add the banana mixture to the flour and stir just enough to incorporate all of the flour. Fold in the chocolate chips.

Line a 10" dinner plate with a piece of parchment paper and turn the dough out on top. Pat it into a disc about 1-inch thick and cover with another piece of parchment paper. Place in freezer for about 30 minutes.

Preheat oven to 400°F. Line a large baking sheet with parchment. Peel off the top layer of parchment paper and invert the scones onto the baking sheet, peeling off the second layer of parchment paper.

Divide the scones into eight wedges and place about ½" apart on the prepared baking sheet. Bake for 25-30 minutes or until the scones are firm to the touch and golden-brown around the edges. Cool completely and cut apart any scones that baked together.

Glaze

In a medium bowl, stir the peanut butter, milk and vanilla together until creamy. Whisk in the confectioners' sugar until smooth. Spoon a small amount of glaze over top of the scones and spread it out with the back of the spoon. Sprinkle with chopped walnuts.

Chocolate Chip Cocoa Scones

2013 Clark County Fair - Deb Dougal - Blue Ribbon

2 cups King Arthur all-purpose flour
1/3 cup cocoa powder
1/3 cup brown sugar
2 tsp. baking powder
¾ tsp. baking soda
1/8 tsp. salt
6 Tbsp. butter, cold, finely diced
1 whole egg

1 cup plain yogurt
½ cup mini chocolate chips
½ tsp. vanilla extract

Glaze:
½ cup powdered sugar, sifted
1 Tbsp. melted butter
1 tsp. vanilla extract
1 tsp. milk

Procedure

Preheat oven to 375°F. Line a baking sheet with parchment paper. In a large bowl, sift together the dry ingredients. With a pastry blender or table knives, cut in the cold butter until mixture resembles coarse meal.

In a small bowl, mix the egg, yogurt, and vanilla. Add to the flour mixture and mix until dough clings together.

Turn out onto floured work surface and knead 10 to 12 times. Do not over work the dough. Divide dough into halves; pat into two circles; cut into shapes. Place about 1-inch apart on prepared baking sheet.

Bake at 375°F or about 18 to 20 minutes or until bottoms are slightly brown. Remove from sheet, cool slightly and glaze.

Glaze

In a small bowl, mix together sifted powdered sugar, melted butter, vanilla extract and milk. Drizzle over tops of scones.

Chocolate Cherry Scones

Blue Ribbon Winner - Oregon State Fair - 2011 Baker: Renata Stanko

2 cups King Arthur unbleached all-purpose flour
¾ tsp. baking soda
1 ½ tsp. cream of tartar
¼ tsp. salt
3 Tbsp. sugar
2 Tbsp. semi-sweet chocolate, ground
7 Tbsp. cold unsalted butter, cut into pieces
¾ cup chopped dried cherries
½ cup semi-sweet chocolate chunks or chips
1 large egg
¾ cup buttermilk

Procedure

Preheat oven to 425°F. Combine flour, baking soda, cream of tartar, salt, sugar and ground chocolate. Cut in the butter. Add cherries and chocolate chips. Combine egg and buttermilk; add to flour mixture. Form into a ball. Place on a floured surface and pat into a circle about ½ inch thick. Cut into 12 wedges; put on prepared baking sheet and bake for about 12 to 14 minutes or until light brown. Makes 12 wedge scones.

Cinnamon Tea Infused Scones

2013 Oregon State Fair - Baker: Mary Folsom

2/3 cup milk
1 teabag Good Earth original tea
2 tsp. vanilla extract
2 cups King Arthur all-purpose flour
¼ cup sugar
1 Tbsp. baking powder

1/8 tsp. salt
½ cup cold butter, finely diced
¼ cup black currants

Glaze
2 Tbsp. milk
2 Tbsp. sugar
½ tsp. cinnamon

Procedure

Bring milk to a simmer over medium heat. Remove from heat and add tea bag. Allow to infuse for 10 minutes. Cool to room temperature, discard teabag and add vanilla extract.

Preheat oven to 400°F. Lightly grease a baking sheet or line with parchment paper.

In a large bowl, combine flour, sugar, baking powder and salt. Cut in the butter until crumbly. Stir in the currants.

Add the tea infused milk to the flour mixture and stir just to combine. Knead just 3 or 4 times.

Divide the dough into 2 pieces and roll or pat each piece into a round disc about ½" thick. Cut each disc into 8 wedges. Place on the prepared baking sheet.

In a small bowl, combine 2 tablespoons sugar and ground cinnamon. Brush tops of scones with milk and sprinkle with cinnamon sugar.

Bake in 400°F oven for 10 to 15 minutes or until lightly browned. Remove to a wire rack to cool.

Recipe Notes

Coconut Lime Scones

2 cups flour
¼ cup sugar
1 Tbsp. baking powder
1 tsp. salt
½ cup cold butter, diced
¼ cup cream
¼ cup. lime juice
2 Tbsp. lime zest
½ tsp. coconut extract

1 tsp. vanilla extract
2 whole eggs, lightly beaten
1 cup sweetened shaved coconut

Coconut Icing
2 cups confectioner's sugar
2 Tbsp. water
½ tsp. coconut extract
Drop green food color

Procedure

Preheat oven to 400°F.

In a large mixing bowl, sift together the flour, sugar, baking powder and salt. Cut in butter until mixture resembles coarse crumbs. Add cream, lime juice, zest and extracts along with eggs and coconut.

Mix until blended. Knead on a floured surface, roll to about ½" thickness and cut with cookie cutter to desired shape. Bake at 400°F for 15 minutes until golden brown. Cool slightly and drizzle with Coconut Icing. Makes about 12 scones.

Coconut Icing

Mix 2 cups confectioner's sugar with two tablespoons water and ½-teaspoon coconut extract.

Cranberry Almond Scones

2012 Oregon State Fair - Baker: Renata Stanko

1 ¼ cup King Arthur unbleached all-purpose flour
¾ cup almond flour
¼ cup sugar
2 tsp. baking powder
½ tsp. salt
½ cup cold butter

½ cup dried cranberries
½ cup slivered almonds
1 whole egg
½ cup cream

For brushing

1 Tbsp. cream
1 Tbsp. sugar

Procedure

Preheat oven to 425°F.

In a bowl, combine King Arthur flour, almond flour, sugar, baking powder and salt. Stir to combine. Cut in butter until mixture resembles coarse crumbs. Stir in cranberries and almonds.

In a small bowl, combine egg and ½ cup cream. Add to flour mixture and stir until just combined. Place dough onto floured surface and form into a ½-inch thick disk with your hands.

Cut into 12 small or 8 medium wedges. Places wedges evenly spaced on ungreased baking sheet. Brush with cream and sprinkle with sugar. Bake at 425°F for 12-15 minutes.

Cranberry and Nut Scones

2012 Clark County Fair - Baker: Irina

3 cups all-purpose flour
½ cup sugar
1 Tbsp. baking powder
½ tsp. baking soda
½ tsp. salt
¾ cup frozen butter
½ cup milk or ½ cup sour cream
1 cup cranberries, coarsely chopped

½ cup walnuts or pecans, chopped
2 tsp. orange peel, grated
1 cup buttermilk

Topping
Additional milk
1 Tbsp. sugar
¼ tsp. cinnamon

Procedure

Preheat oven to 400°F. Lightly grease a large baking sheet.

Sift together the flour, sugar, baking powder, soda and salt. With a pastry blender, cut in the butter until mixture resembles coarse crumbs.

Stir in cranberries, walnuts or pecans and finely grated orange peel. Stir in the buttermilk with a fork just until dry ingredients are moistened.

On a floured surface, roll or pat dough into a ¾-inch thick circle. Cut into rounds with a 2 ½-inch biscuit cutter. Place rounds on a large greased baking sheet, about 1 ½" to 2" apart.

Brush scones with milk or evaporated milk. Combine 1 Tablespoon sugar and ¼ teaspoon cinnamon; sprinkle a little of the sugar mixture over each scone.

Bake for about 15 minutes or until lightly browned. Makes 12 large or 24 medium scones.

Cranberry Island Scones

2013 Oregon State Fair - Baker: Susan Middleton

1 ½ cups King Arthur unbleached all-purpose flour
½ cup King Arthur white whole-wheat flour
1 Tbsp. baking powder
½ tsp. salt
½ tsp. baking soda
1/3 cup sugar
¾ cup dried cranberries

¾ cup dried pineapple chunks, diced
1/3 cup coconut flakes
½ cup cold butter, finely diced
1 whole egg, beaten
2 tsp. vanilla extract
6 oz. pineapple Greek yogurt

Procedure

Preheat oven to 350°F. Lightly grease a baking sheet or line with parchment paper. In a large mixing bowl, sift together the dry ingredients. Add butter cubes to flour mixture and work in the butter with a pastry blender until butter bits are evenly mixed with flour. Add cranberries, pineapple bits and coconut to flour mixture. Mix well.

In a small bowl, beat egg and add vanilla extract and pineapple yogurt; mix well. Gently fold yogurt mixture into dry ingredients, stirring until it holds together. Using an ice cream scoop or a cookie scoop, drop dough onto prepared baking sheet. Bake at 350°F for about 15 minutes or until lightly browned.

Comment: American Indians enjoyed cranberries cooked and sweetened with honey or maple syrup—a cranberry sauce recipe that was likely a treat at early New England Thanksgiving feasts.

By the beginning of the 18th century, the tart red berries were already being exported to England by the colonists.

Cranberries were also used by the Indians decoratively, as a source of red dye and, medicinally, as a poultice for wounds since not only do their astringent tannins contract tissues and help stop bleeding, but we now also know that compounds in cranberries have antibiotic effects.

Cranberry cultivation spread not only across the U.S. through Wisconsin to Washington and Oregon, but also across the sea to Scandinavia and Great Britain.

The hardy berries arrived in Holland as survivors of a shipwreck. When an American ship loaded with crates filled with cranberries sank along the Dutch coast, many crates washed ashore on the small island of Terschelling; some of the berries took root, and cranberries have been cultivated there ever since. *Source: WH Foods*

Cranberry Orange Scones

2013 Blue Ribbon Winner - Clark County Fair - Youth - Baker: Becca Dougal

3 cups King Arthur all-purpose flour
2 ½ tsp. baking powder
½ tsp. baking soda
½ cup sugar
1 tsp. salt
1 Tbsp. orange zest
½ cup chilled butter, finely diced

1 cup dried cranberries
½ cup orange juice
½ cup plain yogurt

Glaze
½ cup powdered sugar, sifted
1 Tbsp. orange juice, plus additional

Procedure

Preheat oven to 400°F. Prepare baking sheet by lining with parchment paper or Silpat. In a large bowl, sift together the dry ingredients.

Cut in the cold butter until mixture resembles coarse crumbs. Add orange zest and cranberries.

In small bowl, combine orange juice and yogurt. Add to dry ingredients, mixing with a fork until moist. Knead about ten times. Do not over work the dough.

On a floured surface, roll into a 9-inch circle and cut into 12 wedges. Place about one or two inches apart onto prepared baking sheet. Bake for about 15 to 20 minutes until tops are golden brown. Transfer to wire rack; drizzle with glaze.

Glaze

In a small bowl, mix powdered sugar with one to two tablespoons orange juice. Drizzle over scones.

Cranberry Orange Scones

Blue Ribbon Winner - Clark County Fair - 2012   Baker: Nataliya Zvozdetskaya

1 ½ cups all-purpose flour
¼ cup sugar
1 Tbsp. baking powder
¼ tsp. salt
¼ cup butter, chilled
½ cup cranberries, coarsely chopped
2 tsp. orange peel, grated
½ cup buttermilk
1 large egg

Glaze:
1 cup powdered sugar, sifted
2 Tbsp. orange juice, plus additional

Procedure

Preheat oven to 400°F. Sift together the flour, ¼-cup sugar, baking powder and salt into a bowl; cut in butter with a pastry blender or fork until mixture resembles coarse crumbs.

Stir in cranberries and orange peel.

In a small bowl, mix buttermilk and egg. Add to dry ingredients all at once, stirring until mixture is just moistened.

On a floured board, knead gently a few times - do not overly knead.

Form into an 8" patty on an ungreased cookie sheet; cut into 8 wedges with a knife but do not move it.

Bake at 400°F for 15 minutes or until light golden.

Mix together powdered sugar and orange juice into a glaze; drizzle over scones.

Cranberry Scones 2011

Blue Ribbon Winner - Oregon State Fair - 2011 Baker: Vicki Cartwright

3 cups King Arthur unbleached all-purpose flour
1/3 cup sugar
2 ½ tsp. baking powder
½ tsp. baking soda
¾ tsp. salt
¾ cup cold butter, finely diced

¾ cup dried cranberries
1 tsp. grated orange peel
1 cup buttermilk

Glaze
1 Tbsp. heavy cream
¼ tsp. ground cinnamon
2 Tbsp. sugar

Procedure

Preheat oven to 400°F. Lightly grease a baking sheet. In a large bowl, sift together the flour, sugar, baking powder, baking soda, and salt. Add the butter and mix until it resembles coarse cornmeal. Add the dried cranberries and orange zest. Pour in the buttermilk and mix until blended. Do not over mix. Gather the dough into a ball and divide in half.

On a floured surface, roll into 2 circles approximately ½ to ¾ inch thick. Cut each circle into 8 wedges. Bake for about 12 to 15 minutes or until golden brown.

Glaze

Combine the cream, cinnamon and sugar in a small bowl until well blended. Set aside while scones are baking. Brush on hot scones.

Cranberry Scones 2012

2012 Clark County Fair - Baker: Snizhana

3 cups all-purpose flour
1/3 cup sugar
1 ½ tsp. baking powder
½ tsp. baking soda
1 tsp. kosher salt
¾ cup unsalted butter
1 cup dried nuts, chopped
1 cup cranberries, coarsely chopped
1 cup buttermilk

Topping
1 tsp. water
1 large egg white, slightly beaten
Extra sugar

Procedure

Preheat oven to 450°F. Lightly grease a cookie sheet. Combine flour, sugar, baking powder, soda and salt in a large bowl. Cut in butter until it is about the size of peas.

Stir in nuts, then the buttermilk all at once. Fold buttermilk and cranberries into the dry mixture until it comes together into a ball.

Dump out onto a floured surface and knead once or twice to bind it all together. Press into a 9" x 15" rectangle. Cut into 15 three-inch squares. Cut each square diagonally so you have 30 triangles. Whisk a teaspoon of water with the egg white and brush over the top of scones. Dust with extra sugar.

Place 2" apart on prepared cookie sheets. Bake at 450°F for 12 minutes or until golden brown.

Cranberry Vanilla Scones

2013 Oregon State Fair - Baker: Mary Folsom

3 cups flour
½ cup + 2 Tbsp. sugar
1 ½ tsp. baking powder
½ tsp. baking soda
½ tsp. salt
6 Tbsp. cold butter
1 ¼ cups milk

1 Tbsp. fresh lemon juice
2 tsp. vanilla extract
1 1/3 cups dried cranberries
milk and sugar to brush tops

Procedure

Preheat oven to 400°F. Lightly grease a baking sheet. In a large bowl, combine flour, sugar, baking powder, baking soda and salt. Cut butter into the flour mixture until it resembles small peas. Stir in the cranberries. In a small bowl, combine the milk and fresh lemon juice.

Add liquid ingredients to the flour mixture all at once and stir with a spoon or spatulas just to combine. Turn dough onto a lightly floured board and press together into a ball. Divide dough into two pieces and pat out each into a flat circle about ½" thick. Cut each circle into 8 wedges. Placed on lightly greased baking sheet.

Bake for 20 minutes or until golden brown. Remove to a rack to cool. Serve slightly warm.

Currant Scones

2012 Blue Ribbon Winner - Clark County Fair - Baker: Ron Palmi

3 cups all-purpose flour
¼ cup sugar
¾ tsp. salt
4 tsp. baking powder
½ cup butter, chilled
1 cup half-and-half
1 cup currants

Glaze:
2 Tbsp. half-and-half
2 tsp. decorating sugar

Procedure

Preheat oven to 375°F. In a bowl, whisk together the flour, sugar, salt and baking powder. Cut in the cold butter until mixture is crumbly.

Stir in half-and-half and currants until just incorporated. Knead in the bowl a few times to bring the dough together.

Turn dough onto a floured surface and press into a circle roughly 9-inches in diameter and 1-inch thick. Cut the dough into 8 wedges. Brush with half-and-half and sprinkle with decorating sugar.

Bake at 375°F until golden brown - about 20-25 minutes.

Dairy Free Coconut Pineapple Scones

2013 Oregon State Fair - Baker: Renata Stanko

2 cups King Arthur unbleached all-purpose flour
¼ cup sugar
2 tsp. baking powder
½ tsp. salt
½ cup cold non-dairy vegan buttery sticks
½ cup chopped dried pineapple
½ cup shredded coconut
½ cup chopped cashews
½ cup unsweetened coconut milk
¼ cup cream of coconut

Procedure

Preheat oven to 400°F. In a bowl, combine flour, sugar, baking powder and salt. Stir to combine. Cut in vegan butter until mixtures has coarse crumbs. Stir in pineapple, coconut and cashews.

In a small bowl, combine coconut milk and cream of coconut. Add coconut liquid to the flour mixture and stir until just combined.

Place dough onto a floured surface and knead a couple of times. Form dough into two ½" thick discs with your hands. Cut each disc into 8 wedges. Place wedges evenly onto an ungreased baking sheet. Bake at 400°F for 10 to 13 minutes.

Dilly Cheese Scones

Blue Ribbon Winner - Oregon State Fair - 2011   Baker: Vicki Cartwright

2 ½ cups King Arthur unbleached all-purpose flour
1 Tbsp. baking powder
2 tsp. dill weed
½ tsp. salt
¾ cup unsalted butter
¼ cup chopped fresh parsley
½ cup shredded cheddar cheese (2 oz.)
½ cup shredded Swiss cheese (2 oz.)
2 whole eggs, lightly beaten
½ cup half-and-half cream

Procedure

Preheat oven to 400°F. Lightly spray a cookie sheet with non-stick cooking spray. Sift together the flour, baking powder, dill weed and salt. Cut in the butter until crumbly. Stir in the fresh parsley and shredded cheeses. Stir in eggs and half-and-half until just moistened.

Turn the dough onto lightly floured surface and knead until smooth. Do not over knead. Divide dough in half. Roll each half into an 8-inch circle. Cut each circle into 8 wedge shapes and place 1" apart on prepared cookie sheet. Bake for 15 to 20 minutes or until lightly browned. Serve hot. Makes 16 wedge shaped scones.

Double Chocolate Scones

2013 Red Ribbon Winner - Clark County Fair - Baker: Matthew Dougal - Youth

2 cups King Arthur unbleached all-purpose flour
1/3 cup cocoa powder
¾ tsp. baking soda
1/3 cup brown sugar
1/8 tsp. salt
2 tsp. baking powder
6 Tbsp. cold butter, finely diced

1 cup vanilla yogurt
½ cup mini chocolate chips

Glaze
½ cup powdered sugar, sifted
1 Tbsp. melted butter
1 tsp. milk
1 tsp. vanilla extract

Procedure

Preheat oven to 375°F. Line baking sheet with parchment paper or Silpat.

In a large bowl, mix together the dry ingredients. Cut in the butter until mixture resembles coarse crumbs.

In a small bowl, mix the vanilla yogurt and egg. Add to flour mixture and stir until dough clings together.

Knead about 10 times. Do not over work the dough. On a floured surface, pat dough into a square and cut into shapes. Bake at 375°F until light brown. Cool on wire rack.

Glaze

Mix powdered sugar, melted butter, milk and vanilla extract until smooth. Spread on top of scones.

Comment: Chocolate has become one of the most popular food types and flavors in the world, and a vast number of foodstuffs involving chocolate have been created.

Chocolate chip cookies have become very common, and very popular, in most parts of Europe and North America. Gifts of chocolate molded into different shapes have become traditional on certain holidays.

Chocolate is also used in cold and hot beverages, to produce chocolate milk and hot chocolate.

Cocoa mass was used originally in Mesoamerica both as a beverage and as an ingredient in foods. Chocolate played a special role in both Maya and Aztec royal and religious events.

Priests presented cacao seeds as offerings to the deities and served chocolate drinks during sacred ceremonies. All of the areas conquered by the Aztecs that grew cacao beans were ordered to pay them as a tax, or as the Aztecs called it, a "tribute".

The Europeans sweetened and fattened it by adding refined sugar and milk, two ingredients unknown to the Mexicans.

By contrast, the Europeans never infused it into their general diet, but have compartmentalized its use to sweets and desserts.

Although cocoa is originally from the Americas, today Western Africa produces almost two-thirds of the world's cocoa. *Source: Wikipedia*

Ginger Pear Drop Scones

1 cup all-purpose flour
1 cup regular or quick-cooking oats
1/3 cup plus 2 teaspoons granulated sugar, divided
1 ½ tsp. baking powder
½ tsp. baking soda
1 tsp. ground ginger
¼ tsp. ground cinnamon
¼ tsp. ground nutmeg
¼ tsp. salt
3 Tbsp. margarine or butter, chilled, cut into small pieces
2/3 cup plain nonfat yogurt
1 whole egg or two egg whites, beaten
1 tsp. vanilla
½ cup finely chopped fresh Bartlett or Bosc pear

Procedure

Heat oven to 400°F. Lightly spray large cookie sheet with non-stick cooking spray.

In a large bowl, combine dry ingredients, reserving 2 teaspoons sugar for topping. Cut in margarine with pastry blender or two knives until mixture resembles coarse crumbs.

In separate bowl, combine yogurt, egg whites and vanilla; mix well. Add to dry ingredients; mix just until moistened. Gently stir in chopped pear until evenly distributed.

Drop by ¼ cupsful onto prepared cookie sheet. Sprinkle 1/8 teaspoon of remaining sugar on each scone.

Bake for 16 to 18 minutes or until light golden brown. Makes 10 drop scones.

Gluten-Free Berry Banana Bonanza Scones

2013 Clark County Fair - Baker: Erica Beauchamp

1 ¾ cups King Arthur Gluten-Free Multi-Purpose Flour
¼ cup sugar
2 tsp. baking powder
½ tsp. xanthan gum
1 stick cold Earth Balance vegan butter
¾ cup blueberries, picked over and washed
¼ cup strawberries -- stemmed and sliced
2 large bananas, peeled and mashed
2 large eggs
1/3 cup cold rice milk
1 tsp. gluten-free vanilla extract

Drizzle
3 Tbsp. honey
2 Tbsp. Earth Balance vegan butter

Filling
2 large bananas, peeled and mashed
½ stick Earth Balance Vegan butter, melted
2 Tbsp. honey

Procedure

Preheat oven to 400°F. Lightly grease a baking sheet. In a bowl, stir together the flour, sugar, baking powder, xanthan gum and salt. Add the vegan butter and blend well. Stir in the blueberries, strawberries and mashed bananas.

47

In a small bowl, lightly beat the eggs; add milk and vanilla. Stir egg mixture into flour mixture. Mix until the dough is sticky.

Drop 8 portions of dough onto the prepared baking sheet and form into triangular shapes. Let sit for 15 minutes.

In a small bowl, stir together 3 tablespoons honey and two tablespoons vegan butter. Drizzle honey butter mixture over scones. Bake for 15 to 20 minutes until golden brown. Remove from oven, cool slightly and cut each in half. Add filling to bottom half and top with upper half.

Filling

In a small bowl, mash the bananas and add melted butter and honey. Mix until there is a thick consistency.

Recipe Notes

Thank you to our sponsor, King Arthur Flour,

King Arthur Flour is America's oldest flour company, founded in Boston in 1790 to provide pure, high-quality flour for residents of the newly formed United States of America.

More than 220 years later, King Arthur Flour is the nation's premier baking resource, offering everything from top-quality baking products to inspiring educational programs—all backed by the passion and commitment of its dedicated employee-owners.

Lavender Cream Scones

Baker: Harriette Hatch

2 cups King Arthur self-rising flour
¼ cup sugar
¼ cup cold butter, diced
2 tsp. dried lavender
1 tsp. fresh lemon zest
½ cup cold heavy whipping cream
1 large egg
½ tsp. vanilla extract

Sugar Glaze
1 cup confectioners' sugar
4 tsp. milk

Procedure

Preheat oven to 350°F. Line a baking sheet with parchment paper or Silpat and set aside.

In a medium bowl, sift together flour and sugar. Cut butter into flour mixture to pea-size or coarse crumbs. Stir in lavender and fresh lemon zest. Set aside.

In a small bowl, whisk together the heavy cream, egg and vanilla extract. Add cream mixture to flour mixture. Stir well. Using hands, bring the dough together.

Turn dough onto a lightly floured surface. Knead lightly 3 to 4 times. Roll dough to ½-inch thickness. With a 2 ¼-inch cookie cutter, cut 12 rounds from dough. Combine scraps, roll and cut more rounds. Place scones on prepared baking sheet.

Bake at 350°F for about 15 minutes or until golden brown. Cool completely on a wire rack. Spread or drizzle Sugar Glaze on cooled scones.

Sugar Glaze

In a small bowl, whisk the confectioners' sugar and milk until smooth and silky. Spread or drizzle on cooled scones.

Mango Ginger Scones

2012 Oregon State Fair - Baker: Renata Stanko

2 cups King Arthur unbleached all-purpose flour
¼ cup sugar
2 tsp. baking powder
½ tsp. salt
½ cup cold butter
½ cup dried mango, chopped

1 Tbs. candied ginger, finely chopped
1 egg white
¼ cup heavy whipping cream (cold)

For brushing tops
2 Tbs. mango juice or nectar
1 Tbs. sugar

Procedure

Preheat oven to 425°F. In a bowl, combine flour, sugar, baking powder and salt. Stir to combine. Cut in butter until mixture resembles coarse crumbs. Stir in mango and ginger.

In a small bowl, combine egg white, cream and mango juice/nectar. Add this liquid to the flour mixture and stir until just combined.

Place dough onto a floured surface and knead a couple of times. Form into a ½-inch thick disc with your hands. Cut into 12 small or 8 medium wedges. Place wedges evenly spaced on ungreased baking sheet. Brush with mango juice and sprinkle with sugar. Bake at 425°F for 13-15 minutes.

51

Maple Glazed Bacon Brickle Scones

2012 Oregon State Fair - Baker: Kathi Karnosh

3 ¼ cups flour
1/3 cup brown sugar
2 ½ tsp. baking powder
½ tsp. baking soda
½ tsp. salt
½ tsp. cinnamon
¼ tsp. nutmeg
¾ cup cold butter
1 cup buttermilk
1 tsp. vanilla
5 whole bacon slices, diced, cooked and drained

¾ cup toffee candy, crushed; (we used Heath's Bits of Brickle)
Additional coarse sugar for sprinkling

Maple Glaze
1 ½ Tbsp. maple syrup
¼ tsp. vanilla extract
Water
1 cup powdered sugar

Procedure

Preheat oven to 425°F. In large bowl, combine dry ingredients. Cut in the butter until it forms coarse crumbs. Stir in buttermilk and vanilla. Fold in bacon crumbles and butter brickle. Turn onto a lightly floured surface and knead gently.

Divide in half and pat into 7-inch round circles. Brush with melted butter and sprinkle with coarse sugar. Cut into 6 or 8 wedges. Bake at 425°F for 12-14 minutes. Top with maple glaze.

Maple Glaze

Combine syrup, vanilla and powdered sugar and stir until combined. Based on the consistency of the glaze, add water one drop at a time and stir. If you accidentally add too much water, just add a bit more powdered sugar. Continue to stir to desired consistency. Brush over scones and serve.

Marionberry Scones

2013 Oregon State Fair - Baker: Julie Wray

2 ½ cups all-purpose flour
1 cup sugar
¾ cup shortening
1 tsp. salt
2 Tbsp. baking powder
½ cup butter
2 cups milk
3 tsp. vanilla extract
1 cup chopped walnuts, divided
2 cups marionberries - fresh or frozen

Procedure

Preheat oven to 375°F. Lightly grease a baking sheet or line with parchment paper. In a mixing bowl, mix the flour, sugar, salt and baking powder. Stir in the shortening until mixture becomes crumbly. Add the butter and milk. Mix in mixer for approximately 1 minute. Fold in vanilla extract, ¾ cup chopped walnuts and marionberries.

With an ice cream scoop or cookie scoop, drop onto prepared baking sheet. Sprinkle with remaining chopped walnuts. Bake at 375°F for about 20 minutes or until golden brown.

Makes a sweet scone or a cake-like berry dessert.

Mixed Berry Scones

2012 Clark County Fair - Baker: Julia

4 ¼ cups all-purpose flour
½ cup sugar
2 Tbsp. baking powder
1 tsp. salt
2 tsp. baking soda
¼ tsp. cinnamon
1 tsp. lemon zest
¾ pound butter, chilled, cubed
3 cups mixed fresh berries (blueberries, raspberries, blackberries)

1 ½ cups buttermilk, chilled

Egg Wash:
1 egg white, slightly beaten
2 Tbsp. milk

Glaze:
½ cup confectioner's sugar
2 tsp. lemon juice
1 tsp. butter
Additional sugar

Procedure

Preheat oven to 400°F and place oven racks in the upper and lower thirds positions. Line two baking sheets with parchment paper.

In the work bowl of a food processor, combine the flour, sugar, and baking powder, salt, cinnamon and lemon zest. Pulse the mixture several times to combine.

Scatter the cold butter pieces over the flour mixture and pulse the processor until the mixture resembles coarse meal. Divide this mixture in half and transfer each half to a medium bowl. Add the berries to one bowl and toss to coat.

Add 2/3 cup buttermilk to each bowl, mixing until just combined and the dough begins to stick together.

Turn the dough with the berries onto a lightly floured work surface and pat into a round about 1" thick. Cut the round into 8 wedges and transfer the wedges to one of the prepared baking sheets. Repeat the process with the remaining dough.

In a separate bowl, slightly beat the egg with the milk. Brush the tops of the scones with the egg wash.

Bake the scones for 12 to 15 minutes switching positions of the baking sheets halfway through, until they are golden brown and firm to the touch. Remove from the oven and allow to rest for 5 minutes.

Prepare the glaze: In a medium microwavable bowl, whisk together the confectioner's sugar and the lemon juice.

Add the lemon zest and the butter. Microwave the mixture in 30-second intervals, stirring after each interval, until the butter has melted.

Spoon the glaze over the warm scones. Sprinkle with sugar. Allow the glaze to set and serve immediately.

Makes 8 large wedge scones or 30 small scones.

Left: Luba Winter during fair booth setup

Shown below: Prize winning recipes - 2011

Moroccan Mint Tea and White Chocolate

2013 Red Ribbon Winner - Oregon State Fair - Baker: Renata Stanko

2 cups King Arthur unbleached all-purpose flour
¼ cup sugar
2 tsp. baking powder
½ tsp. salt
1 tsp. ground cardamom
½ cup cold butter, finely diced
½ cup chopped white chocolate
¼ cup fresh chopped mint
1 egg white
½ cup heavy cream
¼ cup strong Moroccan mint tea

Procedure

Preheat oven to 400°F. In a large bowl, combine flour, sugar, baking powder, salt and cardamom. Stir to combine. Cut in butter until mixture resembles coarse crumbs. Stir in chopped chocolate and fresh chopped mint.

In a small bowl, combine egg white, heavy cream and liquid tea. Add this liquid to the flour mixture and stir until just combined.

Place dough onto a floured surface and knead a couple of times. With your hands, form dough into two ½-inch thick discs. Cut each disc into 8 wedges. Place evenly spaced on ungreased baking sheet. Bake at 400°F for 12 to 15 minutes.

Orange Cranberry Scones

Baker: Harriette Hatch

1 ½ cups all-purpose flour
¼ cup sugar
1 Tbsp. baking powder
¼ tsp. salt
¼ cup cold butter, finely diced
½ cup dried cranberries
2 tsp. grated orange peel

½ cup buttermilk
1 whole egg

GLAZE
1 cup powdered sugar, sifted
3 Tbs. orange juice
1 tsp. grated orange peel

Procedure

Preheat oven to 400°F. Sift together flour, sugar, baking powder and salt in a medium bowl. Cut in butter until mixture resembles coarse crumbs. Stir in cranberries and orange peel.

In a small bowl, mix buttermilk and egg. Add to dry ingredients all at once. Stir until mixture is just moistened.

On a floured surface, knead gently a few times. Do not over work. Form into an 8-inch round on an ungreased cookie sheet. Cut into 8 wedges. Do not move the wedges.

Bake at 400°F for 15-20 minutes or until light golden brown. Remove from oven and cool slightly before drizzling with glaze.

GLAZE

Mix the confectioners' sugar, orange juice and grated orange peel. Drizzle over scones. Separate scones and serve warm.

Below L-R: Harriette Hatch and Jennifer Petersen

Recipe Notes

Orange Rosemary Cranberry Scones

2013 White Ribbon Winner - Oregon State Fair - Baker: Renata Stanko

2 cups King Arthur unbleached all-purpose flour
¼ cup sugar
2 tsp. baking powder
½ tsp. salt
½ cup cold unsalted butter
1 Tbsp. fresh orange zest
1 Tbsp. fresh chopped rosemary
½ cup dried cranberries
¼ cup frozen and thawed orange concentrate
¼ cup heavy cream
1 whole egg
1 Tbsp. orange marmalade
¼ tsp. orange oil

Procedure

Preheat oven to 400°F. In a bowl, combine flour, sugar, baking powder and salt. Stir to combine. Cut in butter until mixture resembles coarse crumbs. Stir in orange zest, finely chopped rosemary and cranberries.

In a small bowl, combine orange concentrate, cream, egg, marmalade and orange oil. Add orange mixture to flour mixture and stir until just combined.

Place dough onto a floured surface and knead a couple of times. Form dough into two ½"-thick discs with your hands. Cut each disc into 8 wedges. Place wedges evenly spaced on ungreased baking sheet. Bake at 400°F for 12 to 15 minutes or until lightly browned.

Potato Griddle Scones

Baker: Harriette Hatch "In Scotland, they are cooked on a griddle and served with breakfast. They have a texture similar to mashed potatoes."

2 large russet potatoes, peeled and diced
6 Tbs. unsalted butter plus 2 extra teaspoons (divided)
1 cup all-purpose flour
½ tsp. baking powder
1 tsp. coarse salt
¼ tsp. black pepper freshly ground
¼ lb. sharp cheddar cheese, grated

Procedure

In a pot of lightly salted boiling water, bring potatoes to a boil. Reduce heat and simmer until fork tender, about 10 to 12 minutes. Drain well.

While still warm, mash potatoes until smooth (you should have 2 ½ cups). Stir 6 tablespoons butter into warm potatoes until well combined.

Stir together flour, baking powder, salt and pepper. Stir dry ingredients into mashed potatoes until just combined.

Form dough into a ball on a lightly floured surface. Cover and let cool for 20 minutes.

Dust rolling pin and work surface with flour. Roll dough into an 8" x 10" rectangle. Gently roll out. With a floured knife, cut dough into four 2 ½" by 4" rectangles and then cut each in half diagonally.

Heat a griddle or non-stick skillet over medium heat and add 1-teaspoon butter. When butter has melted and is bubbly, cook 4 scones until golden brown and cheese melts - about 3 or 4 minutes per side. Keep scones warm in oven while you cook the second group of scones. Serve hot.

Petite Vanilla Bean Scones

2012 Blue Ribbon Winner - Clark County Fair - Baker: Natalia Zagakuk - Professional

2 cups all-purpose flour
1 ½ tsp. baking powder
1/3 tsp. salt
½ cup butter
1/3 cup sugar

½ whole vanilla bean or 2 tsp. vanilla extract
½ cup milk

Glaze:
½ cup confectioner's sugar
2 Tbsp. milk

Procedure

Preheat oven to 400°F. Line a baking sheet with parchment paper. In a medium bowl, whisk together flour, baking powder and salt. In a large bowl, cream together the butter and sugar until light and fluffy.

Cut vanilla bean in half lengthwise and scrape seeds out with a small, sharp knife. Add to butter and sugar mixture and beat to incorporate.

Mix in half of the flour mixture followed by the milk. Stir in remaining flour mixture until dough comes together into a firm, slightly sticky mass.

Divide dough into 5 equal pieces and roll into tennis ball sized rounds. Place on a lightly floured surface and flatten each ball into a disc about ½" to ¾" thick.

After all balls are flattened, cut each into quarters and arrange on prepared baking sheet. Bake for 11 to 15 minutes or until scones are light golden at the edges. Cool on a wire rack before glazing.

GLAZE

Mix together confectioner's sugar and milk until well blended. Drizzle over cooled scones.

Makes 20 wedge scones.

Pumpkin Scones with Cinnamon Glaze

2011 Clark County Fair

1 cup all-purpose flour
1 cup cake flour
1 ½ tsp. baking powder
½ tsp. salt
½ tsp. ground cinnamon
½ tsp. ground nutmeg
¼ tsp. ground allspice
¼ tsp. ground ginger
6 Tbsp. unsalted butter

1/3 cup pumpkin puree
1/3 cup heavy cream
6 Tbsp. brown sugar
1 tsp. vanilla

Glaze
1 cup powdered sugar
2 Tbsp. milk
½ tsp. cinnamon

Procedure

Preheat oven to 425°F. Line baking sheet with parchment paper or line with Silpat. Cut the butter into small pieces and keep refrigerated until ready to use. In a medium bowl, sift together flour, baking powder, salt, and spices. Place bowl in freezer.

In a separate bowl, combine pumpkin, heavy cream, brown sugar, and vanilla and mix well to combine. Refrigerate to keep cold.

Using a pastry blender, cut the butter into the flour mixture until it resembles coarse crumbs. Add cold pumpkin mixture and stir until dough is just moistened. The dough will be very crumbly. Turn the mixture out onto the counter and round into a ball. It should stick together fairly well. Knead it just a couple of times until it starts to come together. Don't over knead - the dough will become too sticky.

Shape the dough into a circle ¾ to 1-inch thick. Cut into 8 wedges. Arrange on prepared baking sheet. Bake for about 15 minutes, or until light brown on the bottom.

Sugar Cinnamon Glaze

Mix together powdered sugar, milk, and cinnamon. Add additional sugar or milk as needed to achieve the desired consistency. Brush or drizzle onto warm scones.

Comment: Pumpkins are believed to have originated in North America. Seeds from related plants have been found in Mexico dating back to 7000 to 5500 B.C. References to pumpkins date back many centuries.

The name pumpkin originated from the Greek word for "large melon" which is "pepon." "Pepon" was changed by the French into "pompon". The English changed "pompon" to "Pumpion".

Native American Indians used pumpkin as a staple in their diets centuries before the pilgrims landed. They also dried strips of pumpkin and wove them into mats.

Indians would also roast long strips of pumpkin on the open fire and eat them. When white settlers arrived, they saw the pumpkins grown by the Indians and pumpkin soon became a staple in their diets. As today, early settlers used them in a wide variety of recipes from desserts to stews and soups.

The origin of pumpkin pie is thought to have occurred when the colonists sliced off the pumpkin top, removed the seeds, and then filled it with milk, spices and honey. The pumpkin was then baked in the hot ashes of a dying fire. Source: The Pumpkin Patch

Amazing Scone Baking Race at Clark County Fair – L-R: Jennifer Petersen, Dale Goff, Brandie Kajino, Luba Winter, Dotty Scott, and Harriette Hatch

Raisin Scones

4 cups all-purpose flour
½ cup sugar
4 tsp. baking powder
½ tsp. baking soda
½ tsp. salt
¾ cup cold unsalted butter, cut into small cubes
½ cup golden raisins
½ cup raisins, currants or chopped dates

1 cup cold heavy whipping cream
2 large eggs
1 Tbsp. vanilla extract
1 Tbsp. grated lemon peel

Brushed Topping
1 egg white, slightly beaten
2 tsp. water

Procedure

Preheat oven to 400°F. Line a large baking sheet with parchment paper or foil. In a large bowl, sift the flour, sugar, baking powder, baking soda and salt. Add butter and mix until mixture resembles coarse meal. Stir in raisins.

In a medium bowl, blend cream, 2 eggs, vanilla and lemon peel. Add egg mixture to flour mixture. Stir until just combined. Gather dough into a ball and knead lightly. Roll out dough on a floured surface to ¾-inch thickness. Using a 2-inch round cookie cutter, cut out scones. Gather scraps, reroll once and cut out additional scones. Place scones on prepared baking sheet, spacing slightly apart.

In a small bowl, whisk remaining egg and 2 teaspoons water to blend. Brush egg mixture over scone tops. Bake at 400°F for about 20 minutes or until golden brown. Transfer scones to rack and cool slightly. Serve warm with butter and marmalade.

Rich Cream Scones

Baker: Harriette Hatch

1 cup cake flour, sifted
2 cups all-purpose flour
½ cup sugar, additional for sprinkling tops
2 tsp. baking powder
½ tsp. baking soda
¾ tsp. salt

¾ cup cold unsalted butter, cut into small cubes
1 ¼ cup cold heavy whipping cream, plus more for brushing
¼ tsp. vanilla extract

Procedure

Preheat oven to 375°F. Line baking sheet with parchment paper or Silpat.

In a large bowl, sift together flours, sugar, baking powder, baking soda and salt. Cut in butter to pea size. With your fingers, flatten butter pieces into small discs. Cover with plastic wrap and refrigerate for one hour to firm the butter bits.

In a small bowl, combine heavy cream and vanilla extract. Stir into flour mixture until almost absorbed and dough just comes together. Turn dough out onto a lightly floured work surface. Roll into an 8" by 10" rectangle. With a short side facing you, fold rectangle into thirds, folding like a letter. Rotate dough a quarter turn clockwise. Repeat rolling out, folding and rotating dough 2 more times. With floured hands, pat dough out to a 1 ¼-inch thickness. Using a 2 ½-inch cookie or biscuit cutter, cut rounds.

Gather scraps, reroll once and cut more rounds (about 12 total).

Place scones 2 inches apart on prepared baking pan. Brush tops with cream and sprinkle with sugar.

Bake at 375°F until golden brown, about 18 to 20 minutes. Serve warm or at room temperature. Makes about 12 round scones.

Spiced Triangles

2011 Clark County Fair - Baker: Duran Gough

3 cups all-purpose flour
1 tsp. baking powder
1 tsp. baking soda
½ cup sugar
2 pouches Alpine apple cider mix
1 tsp. ground cinnamon or apple pie spice
¼ tsp. ground cloves
1 pinch salt
½ cup cold butter, finely diced
¼ cup maple syrup
2/3 cup milk

Procedure

Preheat oven to 375°F. In a mixing bowl, sift together the dry ingredients. With a wire whisk, add the diced cold butter and whisk thoroughly until mixture looks like cornmeal (do not over mix).

In a measuring cup, add the milk and maple syrup; mix together in the measuring cup and then pour mixture into the dry ingredients. Mix together until everything just comes together. Divide into two portions and roll into balls. Flatten balls into rounds that are about ½" thick. Cut rounds into 6 equally portioned triangles.

Flip and place onto an ungreased baking sheet. Bake in preheated oven for about 20 minutes or until an inserted toothpick comes out clean. Makes 12 wedge scones.

Sugar Free Afternoon Delight

2013 Clark County Fair - Baker: Leora Peterson

2 cups King Arthur all-purpose flour
1 Tbsp. baking powder
½ tsp. baking soda
¼ tsp. salt
2 tsp. stevia powder
¼ tsp. cayenne
3 Tbsp. cold butter, diced
¾ cup extra sharp cheddar cheese shredded, divided
¾ cup buttermilk

2 whole eggs
1 cup bacon; cooked, crumbled and drained plus
1 tablespoons
¼ cup Walla Walla sweet onions, peeled and chopped
1 Tbsp. chopped chives, divided
2 tsp. rosemary, fresh chopped

Procedure

Preheat oven to 450°F. Lightly grease baking sheet or line with parchment paper. In a small dish, reserve 1-tablespoon bacon bits and 1 tablespoon chopped chives.

In a large bowl, sift the dry ingredients together. Add butter and blend until mixture resembles coarse crumbs. Stir in ½ cup grated extra sharp cheddar cheese.

In a small bowl, lightly beat eggs then stir in milk. Stir in Walla Walla onions, chopped chives and chopped rosemary.

Add milk mixture to flour mixture until just blended. Turn dough onto floured surface; knead lightly one or two times; shape into a round about ½" thick.

Place on prepared baking sheet, sprinkle a small amount of the remaining ¼ cup grated cheese and reserved chives and bacon bits to the tops. Bake at 450°F for 12 minutes or until golden brown.

Sweet and Spicy Chai Tea Scones

2013 Oregon State Fair - Honorable Mention - Baker: Janet Wheeler

4 cups King Arthur 100% whole wheat flour
4 tsp. baking powder
1 tsp. cinnamon
1 tsp. nutmeg
½ tsp. ground cloves
½ tsp. ground ginger
½ tsp. sea salt
4 Sweet and Spicy chai teabag contents
½ cup cold butter, finely diced
1 cup Greek-style honey yogurt

1 cup chai latté liquid creamer
1/3 cup brown sugar, packed
2 tsp. vanilla extract

Glaze
1 cup confectioner's sugar, sifted
1 tsp. instant coffee granules
2 Tbsp. liquid chai creamer, divided
1 tsp. chai powder beverage mix

Procedure

Preheat oven to 425°F. Lightly grease two 8" pie pans. Mix together flour, baking powder, spices, salt and contents of tea bags. Cut in cold butter. Mixture will be dry and crumbly.

In a separate bowl, combine yogurt, creamer, brown sugar and vanilla. Add yogurt mixture to flour mixture and gently mix.

Divide dough into halves. Place each half into lightly greased 8" pie pans. Pat dough to 1" thickness and smooth sides. Score tops of fresh dough into 12 total scones. Do not separate sections completely.

Bake at 425°F for 25-30 minutes or until top is light brown. Cool on wire rack.

Glaze

In a medium bowl, sift one cup of confectioner's sugar. In a smaller bowl, thoroughly mix instant coffee granules, chai powder beverage mix with one-tablespoon liquid chai creamer. Add coffee/chai mix into the confectioner's sugar. If mixture is too thick, add a few drops of second tablespoon of liquid chai creamer to glaze. Separate scones and drizzle tops of scones allowing some to drip down the sides. Delicious with tea or coffee.

Judging at Clark County Fair:
Above: Harriette Hatch and Pat Jollota
Below: Brandie Kajino and Jennifer Petersen

Strawberry Scones

2011 Winner Oregon State Fair - Baker: Susan Middleton

1 ¼ cups King Arthur unbleached all-purpose flour
1 cup King Arthur white whole-wheat flour
1 Tbsp. baking powder
½ tsp. salt
1/3 cup sugar
½ cup butter
1 cup vanilla chips
1 whole egg beaten

1 tsp. vanilla
½ box 3.5 oz. instant strawberry pudding mix
½ tsp. baking soda
2/3 cup 1% milk
½ cup plain Greek yogurt
¾ cup diced strawberries

Glaze
1 cup confectioners' sugar
1 Tbsp. water

Procedure

Preheat oven to 350°F. Dice cold butter into small pieces and set aside. Sift flours, baking powder, salt and sugar into a large bowl. Mix pudding mix, milk, baking soda, yogurt in a small bowl. Add beaten egg and vanilla and mix well. Cut butter into flour mixture until it resembles coarse crumbs. Stir in vanilla chips. Make a well in center and add pudding mixture. Knead 10-12 times on floured surface. Divide in half.

Roll one-half of dough into a circle ½-inch thick. Spoon diced strawberries onto circle. Roll second half of dough into circle and place on top of first layer with strawberries. Press lightly together. Cut into 12 pie shapes with pizza cutter. Place on large cookie sheet leaving ½-inch space between each. Lightly baste scones with milk.

Bake at 350 degrees for 20 minutes or until lightly browned.

Glaze

Mix confectioners' sugar and water until smooth. Drizzle over scones.

Sugar Free Pumpkin Scones

Blue Ribbon - Oregon State Fair - 2011 Baker: Renata Stanko

2 cups King Arthur unbleached all-purpose flour
7 Tbsp. Splenda or sugar substitute
1 Tbsp. baking powder
½ tsp. salt
½ tsp. ground cinnamon
½ tsp. ground nutmeg
¼ tsp. ground cloves
¼ tsp. ground ginger
6 Tbsp. unsalted butter, cold and diced
½ cup pumpkin puree
3 Tbsp. cream
1 large egg

Procedure

Preheat oven to 425°F. Sift together flour, Splenda, baking powder, salt and spices. Cut in butter until crumbly. Combine pumpkin, cream and egg. Add to flour mixture and form into a ball. Place on floured surface and pat into a circle ½ inch thick. Cut into 12 wedges. Bake at 425°F for 10-12 minutes. Makes 12 wedge scones.

Sweet Nutty Bing

2011 Clark County Fair - Baker: Duran Gough

3 cups all-purpose flour
1 tsp. baking powder
1 tsp. baking soda
½ cup sugar
¾ cup pistachios, chopped
1 pinch salt
½ cup cold butter, finely diced
1 cup Bing black cherries, pitted, chopped
2/3 cup milk
1 cup semi-sweet chocolate (four 1 ounce squares), ground

Procedure

Preheat oven to 375°F. In a mixing bowl, sift together the dry ingredients. With a wire whisk, thoroughly mix the diced cold butter into the dry mixture until mixture looks like cornmeal (do not over mix).

Add the cherries and then add the milk until everything just comes together. Divide into 2 portions, roll into balls and flatten into rounds about ½" thick. Cut each round into 6 equal-portion triangles.

Flip and place pieces onto an ungreased baking sheet. Sprinkle with ground dark chocolate. Bake for about 20 minutes or until an inserted toothpick comes out clean.

Makes 12 wedge scones.

The White Pumpkin

2011 Blue Ribbon Winner - Clark County Fair - Junior Division   Baker: Maya Gough

3 cups all-purpose flour
1 tsp. baking powder
1 tsp. baking soda
2 tsp. ground cinnamon
½ cup white chocolate - ground
¼ cup sugar
1 pinch salt
½ cup cold butter, finely diced
2/3 cup pumpkin, cooked
¼ cup milk

Topping
¼ cup pumpkin seeds
1 Tbsp. raw sugar

Procedure

Preheat oven to 375°F. In a mixing bowl, sift together the dry ingredients. With a wire whisk, thoroughly mix cut butter into the dry mixture until mixture looks like cornmeal (do not over mix).

In a small mixing bowl, add the ¼-cup milk, the 2/3 cup pumpkin - mix them together and then pour into the dry ingredients. Mix until everything just comes together. Divide into two equal portions and roll into balls. Sprinkle working surface with raw sugar and pumpkin seeds; place dough balls on top of mixture and press into rounds about ½" thick. Cut each round into six equal portion triangles.

Flip and place pieces on an ungreased baking sheet (with raw sugar and pumpkin seeds on top). Bake for about 20 minutes or until an inserted toothpick comes out clean.

Winter Spice Scones

4 cups self-rising flour
3 Tbsp. superfine sugar
1 pinch salt
3 Tbsp. butter
1 cup milk
3 Tbsp. orange marmalade
1 tsp. freshly ground
cardamom seeds

Glaze
¼ cup orange marmalade

2 Tbsp. water
1 tsp. freshly ground
cardamom seeds
1 Tbsp. orange zest

Mascarpone Cream
1 Tbsp. orange blossom
water
1 Tbsp. honey
1 cup plus 1-tablespoon
mascarpone

Procedure

Scones

Sift the flour, sugar, and salt into a bowl. Cut the butter into small chunks and add it to the flour mixture; use a fork to work the mixture into a crumbly dough. Add the milk, marmalade, and cardamom. Work the mixture quickly and lightly into a smooth dough. Don't knead too long or the scones will be tough.

On a lightly floured surface, roll out the dough to ¾-inch thick. With a cookie cutter, cut 1 ½-inch rounds. Place them on a baking sheet lined with parchment paper. Combine the scraps, roll dough and cut more rounds.

Let the scones chill for 15 minutes or overnight in the refrigerator.

Preheat the oven to 450°F. Bake for 12 to 15 minutes or until golden brown. Cool slightly and brush with glaze.

Glaze

In a saucepan, heat the marmalade with 2 Tablespoons water, stir in the cardamom, then press the mixture through a sieve into a bowl. Brush the scones with the syrup and sprinkle them with the orange zest.

Mascarpone Cream

Fold the orange blossom water and honey into the mascarpone and whip until fluffy. Serve the scones with the mascarpone cream. Makes 12 scones.

Comment: Mascarpone is a very rich Italian cheese concentrated from milk cream and has a fat content of up to 75%. It has a very smooth, creamy, and sweet texture. Mascarpone Cream is a combination of mascarpone with zabaglione and whipped cream.

Mascarpone cheese can be hard to find. Here's an easy mock mascarpone recipe to make at home.

Mock Mascarpone

1 pint heavy cream
1 ½ teaspoons cream of tartar

Directions:

1. Pour cream into a metal bowl, and place over a pan of simmering water. Heat until warm. Stir in the cream of tartar, and continue to heat and stir until the temperature reaches 180 degrees F. Remove from heat.

2. Line a colander or strainer with cheesecloth, and place over a bowl. Pour mixture into the strainer and let drain overnight in the refrigerator. Scoop the cheese into a covered container and store in the refrigerator for up to one week.

Venice Yummli Scones

2012 Winner - Clark County Fair - Baker: Oksana Globak

5 cups all-purpose flour
1 ½ tsp. baking powder
1/3 tsp. salt
2 cups sugar
½ cup butter, at room temperature
½ whole vanilla bean or 2 tsp. vanilla extract
½ cup milk
2 cups heavy whipping cream (cold)
4 whole eggs slightly beaten
2 cups cranberries, coarsely chopped

Procedure

Preheat oven to 400°F. Lightly grease a baking sheet.

Blend flour, baking powder, salt and sugar in food processor. Add butter by pulsing the processor on and off until mixture resembles coarse meal.

Remove from food processor and put into large bowl.

In a separate bowl, mix the cream and beaten eggs. Make a well in the center and add the cream/egg mixture. Using a fork, stir until just moistened. Stir in the cranberries.

Place dough on a floured surface or onto floured wax paper. Gently knead until smooth, about 6 or 8 times. Divide dough into halves. Pat each half into a ¾" thick round.

Cut each round into 6 wedges (like when cutting a pie). Place the wedges on a lightly greased baking sheet, spacing them about 1" apart.

Bake scones at 400°F until light brown, about 18 minutes.

Cool completely or grab a cuppa coffee or tea and eat one while still warm.

Victorian Currant Scones

2 cups King Arthur all-purpose flour
4 tsp. baking powder
¾ tsp. salt
1/3 cup sugar
4 Tbsp. butter
2 Tbsp. shortening
¾ cup cream
1 egg
½ cup dried currants or dried cranberries

Procedure

Heat oven to 375°F.

In a large mixing bowl, combine flour, baking powder, salt and sugar. Mix well. Cut in butter and shortening. In a separate bowl, combine cream and egg. Add all at once to dry ingredients. Add fruit and mix lightly.

Turn dough out onto a floured surface. Roll dough to about ½" thick and cut into biscuit size rounds. Bake at 375°F for 15 minutes or until brown. Makes 12 round scones.

Amazing Scone Baking Race at Oregon State Fair:
L-R: Jennifer Petersen, Marilyn Miller, Janet Ellis

Recipe Notes

Recipe Name: _____

Source: _____

Ingredients: _____

Oven Temp: _____

_____

Directions _____

_____

_____

_____

_____

_____

_____

Recipe Name: _____

Source: _____

Ingredients: _____

Oven Temp: _____

_____

Directions _____

_____

_____

_____

_____

_____

_____

Recipe Notes

Recipe Name: Source:

Ingredients: Oven Temp:

Directions

Recipe Name: Source:

Ingredients: Oven Temp:

Directions

Conversion Charts

U S Dry Volume Measurements

MEASURE	EQUALS
1/16 teaspoon	dash
1/8 teaspoon	a pinch
3 teaspoons	1 Tablespoon
1/8 cup	2 Tablespoons
¼ cup	4 Tablespoons
1/3 cup	5 Tablespoons plus 1 teaspoon
½ cup	8 Tablespoons
¾ cup	12 Tablespoons
1 cup	16 Tablespoons
1 pound	16 ounces

U S Liquid Volume Measurements

MEASURE	EQUALS	EQUALS2
1 Cup		8 fluid ounces
1 Pint	2 Cups	16 fluid ounces
1 Quart	2 Pints	4 cups
1 Gallon	4 Quarts	16 cups

U S to Metric Conversions

MEASURE	EQUALS
1/5 teaspoon	1 ml
1 teaspoon	5 ml
1 Tablespoon	15 ml
1 fluid oz.	30 ml
1/5 cup	50 ml
1 cup	240 ml
2 cups (1 pint)	470 ml
4 cups (1 quart)	.95 liter
4 quarts (1 gallon)	3.8 liters
1 oz.	28 grams
1 pound	454 grams

Pan Size Equivalents

MEASURE	EQUALS
9" x 13" baking pan	22cm x 33cm baking pan
8" x 8" baking pan	20cm x 20cm baking pan
9" x 5" loaf pan	23cm x 12 cm loaf pan
9" cake pan	22cm cake pan
10" tart or cake pan	25cm tart or cake pan

Ratios for Various Foods

MEASURE	EQUALS	EQUALS2
BUTTER		
1 Tbsp.	1 Tablespoon	14g
1 stick	4 ounces	113g
4 sticks = 1 pound	1 pound	452g
LEMON		
1 lemon	1 to 3 Tablespoons Juice	1½ teaspoons grated zest
4 large lemons	1 cup juice	¼ cup grated zest
CHOCOLATE		
1 ounce	¼ cup grated	40g
6 ounces chocolate chips	1 cup chocolate chips	160g
4.2 ounces cocoa powder	1 cup cocoa powder	118g

Creams - Butterfat Value

Milk Product	Other Name	Butterfat %
Half-and-half	Half milk, half cream	10.5% to 18% butterfat
Light cream		18% butterfat
Light whipping cream		26-30% butterfat
Heavy cream	Whipping cream	36% or more butterfat
Double cream	Clotted cream or Devonshire cream	42% butterfat

Oven Temperature Conversions

FAHRENHEIT	CELSIUS	GAS MARK
275°F	140° C	1-Cool
300°F	150° C	2
325°F	165° C	3-Very Moderate
350°F	180° C	4-Moderate
375°F	190° C	5
400°F	200° C	6-Moderately Hot
425°F	220° C	7-Hot
450°F	230° C	9
475°F	240° C	10-Very Hot

We appreciate our sponsors!

Please remember to visit our sponsors.

King Arthur Flour   Thistledown Cozies

17-76 Tea Party Cookbook   Fresh Cup Magazine

Aevum Images   Chariteas   Nu Way Beauty

Judges: Clark County Fair

Harriette Hatch, Pat Jollota, Kate Singh (Aevum Images), Brandie Kajino, Dotty Scott, Luba Winter, J.R. Holt, Jr.

Judges – Oregon State Fair

Charity Chalmers, Kate Singh, Marilyn Miller, Janet Ellis, Winnie Broderick, Jan Weigel

Celebrate the Season With A Refreshing Idea!

If summertime, wintertime or anytime the season changes and it gives you the hot tea blues, try the Amazing Scone

Baking Race to cook up a baking and tea event at your local teashop, coffee shop, bakery or state fair!

Join the Amazing Scone Baking Race!

Enter the CONTEST to win one of many incredible prizes for scone bakers.

You can host a contest at your location, use it for an organization fund-raiser, and feature it at your local fair or trade show event and more.

Visit the Amazing Scone Baking Race website to learn more about participating in the contest either as a baker or as a host.

Like to see the Amazing Scone Baking Race at your favorite event? Ask them to contact us for details at tea@teatrademart.com. We'd love to make the connection and we'll keep you in the loop.

Book Review

Please take a few moments to review on Amazon.

Scone Recipes: Amazing Scone Baking Race

Jennifer loves to hear from her readers and to share recipes.

Rather read the blog on your Kindle?
Blog: Over the Teacups http://www.overtheteacups.com

Facebook: Amazing Scones Baking Race

Twitter – http://www.twitter.com/amazing_scones

Jennifer's Pinterest: jpetersen01

For photos of the recipes in this cookbook, please go to our Pinterest page.

To receive free recipes and advance notice of future books by Jennifer Petersen, please visit our other website http://www.teatrademart.com.

Thank you for purchasing the Amazing Scone Baking Contest recipe collection!

Made in the USA
Lexington, KY
19 January 2015